Careers in Forensics ™

Careers as a
Medical Examiner

Fig. A

Corona Brezina

rosen publishing's
rosen
central

New York

Published in 2008 by The Rosen Publishing Group, Inc.
29 East 21st Street, New York, NY 10010

First Edition

Library of Congress Cataloging-in-Publication Data

Brezina, Corona.
Careers as a medical examiner / Corona Brezina.
   p. cm.—(Careers in forensics)
Includes bibliographical references and index.
ISBN-13: 978-1-4042-1347-0 (library binding)
1. Medical examiners (Law)—Vocational guidance—Juvenile literature.
2. Forensic pathology—Vocational guidance—Juvenile literature. 3. Forensic sciences—Vocational guidance—Juvenile literature. I. Title.
RA1063.4.B74 2008
614'.1023—dc22

          2007034106

Manufactured in the United States of America

On the cover: Hazmat personnel, a DNA lab technician and forensic scientist, and a chief medical doctor in a New York medical examiner's office.

Contents

Television crime dramas such as the *CSI* franchise offer viewers a riveting look into the world of criminal science and forensics. Thanks to such programs, viewers have become increasingly savvy about investigative matters such as securing a crime scene, collecting different types of trace evidence, checking fingerprint databases, and identifying DNA matches. *CSI* and similar shows—and even news coverage on the forensic angle of some real-life crimes—have turned the field of forensics into a subject of public fascination.

Forensic science can be broadly defined as the application of scientific tools and procedures to legal matters, particularly if a crime has been committed or an unusual death has occurred. It is a vast discipline that incorporates a broad range of different sciences and areas of specialization. These include many fields that are relevant for obvious reasons, such as medicine, anthropology, odontology (dentistry/bite mark evidence), entomology (the examination of insects associated with decomposing human remains), biology, psychology, and chemistry. Surprisingly, there are forensic applications of accounting, engineering, art, linguistics, mathematics, seismology (the study of earthquakes and seismic waves), and many other diverse areas. These are only a few of the fields with potential tie-ins to forensics.

A single crime scene can yield evidence requiring the expertise of forensic experts in a variety of disciplines. There may be fingerprints, footmarks, pools of blood, blood spatter patterns, bullets, documents shedding light on the crime or its motive, trace evidence such as hairs or fibers, paint chips, broken glass, insects, or pollen. Technicians photograph the scene and gather evidence for later

A forensics technician checks for the presence of blood on a bedroom floor. Crime scene investigators wear protective gear to avoid contaminating evidence—and for their own safety.

examination and analysis in the laboratory. They must document each item and take precautions to avoid contaminating the scene or any piece of evidence.

In the case of a suspicious or unexpected death, the body is often the most important piece of evidence at the crime scene.

Investigators from the medical examiner's office survey the scene where a small plane crashed into an automobile body shop in Atlanta, Georgia, shortly after takeoff. The two people aboard the plane were killed.

Investigating the body is the duty of the medical examiner (ME). An investigator from the ME's office examines the body at the scene of the crime, and then it is transported to the ME's office for a thorough examination, which includes an autopsy.

MEs are doctors who have been trained in the field of forensic pathology. Pathology is the medical specialty concerned with the study and diagnosis of disease and injuries. Forensic pathologists, therefore, are experts in determining how an illness or injury led to a possibly criminal death, one in which foul play is suspected. From what they learn during their investigations into suspicious or unexpected deaths, medical examiners are able to help serve justice on behalf of the dead. Since their work sometimes reveals ways of preventing future needless deaths, medical examiners also use their knowledge to help the living.

Though the ME's work occurs behind closed doors, away from the rush and excitement of the crime scene, active police investigation, and media glare, it is a fascinating, rewarding, and noble career. Medical examiners play a crucial role in creating a society built upon justice and safety. This book will introduce you to the field and provide you with the information you need in order to determine if it is the kind of work that appeals to you. If your interest in the field remains strong, this book will also serve as your guide to building a solid, successful, and enduring career in forensic pathology.

Emergency Call:
Examination at Ground Zero

September 11, 2001, began quietly, a sunny, beautiful late summer day. In New York City's Office of Chief Medical Examiner (OCME), the daily routine of meetings and lab work had just started when the fire alarm went off around 8:45 AM. Early reports informed the office that a small plane had hit the World Trade Center. The reports soon changed, however, to say that two large hijacked passenger jets had intentionally crashed into both towers of the World Trade Center. What had sounded like a relatively small accident had suddenly turned into a major and deliberate terrorist attack, possibly involving hundreds or even thousands of dead and injured people. Within minutes, the World Trade Center had become one of the largest crime scenes in history.

The OCME reacted quickly. The chief medical examiner himself, Dr. Charles Hirsch, led a team of OCME workers to the site. There they planned to check out the scope of the destruction, relay information back to the office, and begin preparing a temporary system for receiving and identifying bodies. The rest of the staff would remain in the office, waiting for instructions to come through Hirsch's radio.

Not long after Hirsch's team arrived at the scene, the first tower collapsed and the radio link went dead. Almost a half hour later, the second tower fell. Back at the OCME, the staff set to work preparing for the arrival of the remains of the disaster victims. It was not until late that afternoon that a bruised and battered Dr. Hirsch returned to the office, having survived getting hit by a piece of falling concrete.

The Office of Chief Medical Examiner

The south tower of the World Trade Center begins to collapse on September 11, 2001, shortly after terrorists crashed into both towers with airliners.

New York City's Office of Chief Medical Examiner is responsible for investigating and examining the body of any person who dies an unusual, unexpected, or violent death within the city limits. Because of the volume of deaths in a city of 8.2 million people, the OCME has forty medical examiners on staff, a greater number of forensic pathologists than those

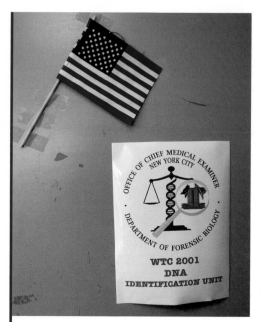

Above is the door to one of the labs in New York City's OCME. After the 9/11 attacks, there was an outpouring of support from volunteers across the country willing to help with the recovery effort.

employed by many entire U.S. states. The MEs typically work in the autopsy rooms while medicolegal investigators (MLIs)—trained physician assistants with additional forensic and legal qualifications—respond to the scene of a death.

The OCME's headquarters in Manhattan is a bustling building located between New York University Hospital and Bellevue Hospital Center. Within it are all of the departments and laboratories necessary for running one of the nation's top medical examiner's offices. There are separate departments for toxicology (the study of the harmful effects of chemicals on living organisms), histology (the study of thin slices of tissue), and serology (testing of blood), as well as a new state-of-the-art forensic biology laboratory that is the nation's largest government-operated DNA laboratory. In 2001, no ME's office in the United States could have been better prepared to handle a mass fatality event than the OCME, but the scale of the World Trade Center disaster was nevertheless overwhelming.

Identifying the Dead

On the afternoon of September 11, several hours after the attacks and the collapse of the twin towers, the OCME began the effort of examining and identifying the remains of the people who died at the World Trade Center and in the hijacked jets. It was an undertaking that would continue for nearly four years.

A few intact bodies were brought in early on in the process, but most of the remains arrived in fragments. From the start, investigators knew that they would not be able to identify remains of every missing person. Some bodies had been essentially vaporized by the force of the initial impact of the planes crashing into the World Trade Center. The ensuing fires reached temperatures as high as 1800° Fahrenheit (982° Celsius). The 110-story towers collapsed in a space of six to nine seconds, reducing the structures to a pile of rubble and crushing everything within and underneath them.

In many previous mass fatality events, such as plane crashes, investigators could work from a passenger list that provided information about where each person had been seated. Following the World Trade Center attacks, there was no way of knowing the identities or even the number of victims. Officials investigating the disaster had to compile an official missing persons list from scratch. The final list included the names of 2,749 people who lost their lives in the World Trade Center attacks. Nearly 20,000 remains, most of them partial, were recovered from the site.

When remains were brought into the OCME, they were first examined by an ME and an anthropologist to confirm that they were human. The ME recorded a thorough description of the remains as well as the exact time and place the remains had been recovered.

Families provided the OCME with data on the missing persons, such as photographs, X-rays, identifying features and jewelry, dental records, and even toothbrushes and hairbrushes (which might provide valuable DNA information). Relatives also gave samples of their own DNA to test for possible matches.

Forensic experts in a number of fields worked to identify the victims. Identifications were made through fingerprints, dental records, personal effects, and even forensic podiatry, in which victims were identified by their feet. Many identifications were "composite IDs," in which several different techniques produced partially usable information. For example, remains discovered at a certain location may have yielded a partial fingerprint, a damaged DNA sample, and a piece of jewelry. None of this evidence on its own would provide a positive identification of a victim. But three corroborating pieces of information found together—personal effects, genetic material, or other unique identifying information—were considered conclusive.

Many remains were so fragmentary that DNA testing provided the only hope for identification. Even so, the DNA was often too

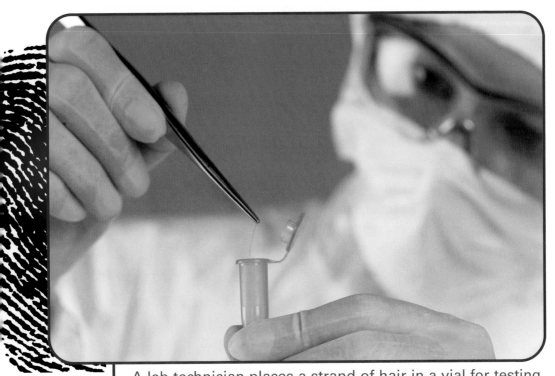

A lab technician places a strand of hair in a vial for testing. Many World Trade Center victims were identified through analysis of DNA recovered from the human remains found in the destroyed buildings' debris.

degraded to provide a match through conventional techniques. In fact, the OCME Forensic Biology Department, in conjunction with federal organizations and private companies, pioneered new DNA technologies in order to identify some of the World Trade Center victims.

New victim identifications gradually slowed, then stopped. In 2005, the OCME formally announced that it had exhausted the limits of current technology in the identification effort. Nearly 1,600 people had been identified, over half of them through DNA analysis.

2 | On the Job

They might get some of the details wrong, but forensic science–themed television shows and other pop culture sources are generally accurate in their portrayal of the medical examiner as one of the most important figures involved in a death investigation. The ME has the responsibility of collecting and evaluating evidence related to the death, performing the autopsy, and reconstructing how the body received its fatal injuries. The ME submits his or her findings in an autopsy report and may later testify as an expert witness if a case goes to court.

A Case for the ME

Medical examiners are called in to investigate any death that is violent, suspicious, or unexpected. These include homicides and possible homicides, suicides and possible suicides, fatal accidents, deaths of prisoners, and occupational (workplace) deaths. The ME also investigates any death that could potentially affect public health, such as a suspected case of tuberculosis, avian flu, or West Nile infection.

Scene investigators secure evidence following a double homicide. Trace evidence can reveal clues that could prove crucial in investigating and prosecuting a criminal case.

An official from the ME's office photographs an accident scene. Bodies will be transported to the ME's office for autopsy.

Not every death requires an autopsy—the ME has the authority to determine the necessary scope of the investigation. Many deaths reported to the ME's office occur in hospitals. In these cases, a telephone interview with the doctor often provides enough information to adequately explain the circumstances of death without further involvement of the ME. If the individual has died after a long battle with terminal cancer, for example, there is no need to continue the investigation.

When a police officer reports finding a body, the ME or a scene investigator working for the ME's office travels to the scene of the death. The most immediate concern is securing the scene in order to preserve evidence that can indicate whether the death was natural, accidental, or intentional, and, if intentional, who may have been the killer. Often, the scene is already compromised by the time the ME arrives. If emergency medical technicians tried to revive the individual, it will affect the state of the body and the surroundings. Witnesses can also inadvertently contaminate potential evidence.

Before laying hands on anything, crime scene investigators measure and sketch the scene, document conditions, and take photographs. Next, forensic technicians collect evidence, and the scene investigator from the ME's office examines the body and the surrounding scene. He or she makes a preliminary estimate of the time of death and offers possible death scenarios based on the available evidence. He or she will then write up a report and determine whether an autopsy is necessary.

The Autopsy

The autopsy—the postmortem examination in which the body is dissected—is central to the death investigation. An ME performs medicolegal autopsies, which serve a different function from autopsies done in hospitals. Hospital autopsies answer questions about the medical issues that resulted in a person's death. Medicolegal autopsies are performed for legal as well as medical purposes. In some cases, the results may be relevant in the courtroom. MEs, who are trained in forensic pathology, have the expertise to reconstruct the circumstances of death based on wounds, sudden and unusual changes in the body, trauma to the body, toxicity of blood, and other internal and external physical evidence.

Every victim of what is suspected to be a criminal fatality undergoes a complete autopsy. A stabbing victim, for instance, will have the top of the skull removed for examination of the brain even though the ME does not suspect any damage to the brain. A body with massive trauma to the head will have the chest opened and internal organs examined. By performing a thorough examination, the ME excludes other possible causes of death that might not have been immediately obvious. Bodies recovered from rivers, for example, are often first assumed to have been accidentally drowned. Yet an autopsy may reveal blunt trauma to the head and lungs free of water, indicating that the victim had stopped breathing before he or she was dumped in the river and was probably killed by a blow to the head. The body was thrown in the river just to make it look like an accidental death or suicide.

The autopsy begins with a visual inspection of the body. The corpse is removed from the body bag or other container and placed on a metal autopsy table. It is examined and photographed, and the ME uses a voice recorder to make notes during the process. If the body is still clothed, it is then undressed and photographed again. The clothing and any trace evidence is preserved for further forensic examination. Pathology assistants help during the autopsy process.

The ME makes note of the body's race, sex, age, hair color, and eye color, as well as any distinguishing features such as birthmarks, deformities, scars, jewelry, and tattoos. A member of the autopsy team takes fingerprints and footprints. The hair is combed for possible evidence, and hair and fingernail samples are collected. The ME examines the mouth and other openings of the body. If deemed necessary, swabs are taken as part of a rape kit to

Dennis Cavalli, medicolegal investigator; Theresa Caragine, DNA lab technician and forensic scientist; Dr. Michele Slone, chief medical doctor; and Frank DePaolo, medicolegal investigator, stand in the autopsy room of New York City's OCME.

determine whether there are traces of semen present in any of the body's orifices, or openings. The ME may examine the body under ultraviolet light or laser lighting in order to detect bruises, fingerprints, and trace evidence that might not be apparent to the naked eye.

Particular attention is paid to signs of injury. Blunt instruments leave bruises and tears in the skin that may yield information about the assault and type of weapon used. If the attacker laid

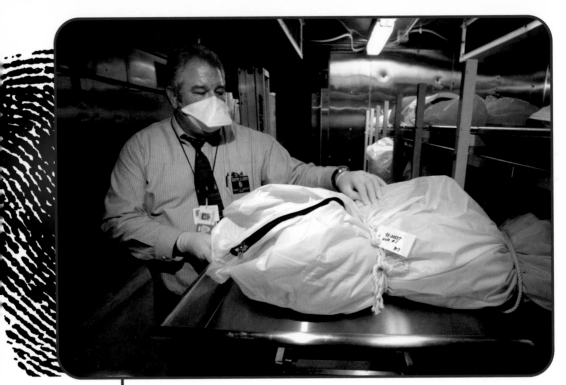

Craig Harvey, chief coroner investigator and chief of operations at the Los Angeles County Coroners Office, examines a body stored in the crypt.

hands on the victim, hand and finger impressions may be visible. The condition of the skin around a bullet wound can reveal whether the weapon was held close to the body or whether the victim was shot from a distance. Entry and exit wounds of bullets can be differentiated. An ME can sometimes determine from a surface inspection of a stab wound whether it was inflicted by a single-edged knife (such as a kitchen knife), a double-edged knife, or some other kind of sharp instrument. The marks left after a strangulation can be used to determine whether a case is a suicide (by hanging or self-asphyxiation) or a murder. Small hemorrhages—internal bleeding—around the eyes are another possible indication of strangulation. A pattern of defensive wounds on hands or arms may show that the victim was trying to fight off an attacker. Marks from hypodermic needles may indicate that the individual was a drug user, which in turn may provide clues about likely suspects.

Some injuries may require a more thorough examination. An X-ray may reveal broken bones and foreign objects, such as bullet fragments, within the body. The ME may take casts of penetration wounds that extend into the body, such as bites and knife wounds. The paths of bullets can be determined by tracing the paths with long metal probes.

The ME begins the internal examination by making a Y-shaped incision along the torso, from the collarbones down to the pubic bone, and pulls back the skin and muscles. He or she then cuts the ribs down each side of the body and removes the front of the ribcage. The internal organs of the body are now visible for examination.

Each organ is removed individually and weighed, beginning with the heart. If an organ is unusually heavy or light, this could be a contributing factor in the individual's death. The ME slices—or "sections"—each organ in order to examine it and takes a sample that may be tested and stored. From the heart, the ME moves on to the liver and other organs, moving down the torso. A diseased

Coroner or ME?

The terms "medical examiner" and "coroner" are not interchangeable. Coroners may be appointed or elected, and they do not have to have any medical or forensic expertise. Sometimes a county's coroner also works as the local funeral director.

The first coroners were knights appointed in 1194 by King Henry II of England, chosen to serve in the countryside as the king's representatives. Their most important task was to investigate violent or suspicious deaths, recording every detail at hand and collecting any fines or fees that the deceased might have owed to the king. In 1637, King Charles I appointed Maryland colony resident Thomas Baldridge the first coroner in what is now the United States. Coroners

The position of coroner dates back to the reign of King Henry II of England. If a medieval coroner ruled that a death was a suicide, the estate of the deceased would be forfeited.

1 2 3 4 5 6 7 8 9 10 11 12 13 14 15 16 17 18 19 20

remained the foremost authorities on death in the United States until 1890, when the city of Baltimore, Maryland, appointed two doctors to serve as medical examiners.

Unlike coroners, medical examiners must hold a degree in medicine. In order to be certified by the American Board of Pathology, they must also undergo intensive training in forensic pathology. In the United States, the medical examiner system has largely replaced the older coroner model. Individual offices can apply for accreditation by the National Association of Medical Examiners. Twenty-two states have a medical examiner system, ten states retain the coroner model, and the remainder have a mixture of the two systems.

liver may indicate that the individual abused alcohol. A smoker's lungs are visibly discolored. The ME can tell whether a female victim has ever given birth. If the ME encounters bone or cartilage that has been scratched or scored by a knife, it is removed for further examination. The contents of the stomach are examined and set aside.

Next, the ME dissects the neck, examines the tongue, and moves on to the head. In order to remove the brain, he or she makes a long incision in the back of the head and pulls the scalp up toward the face, exposing the skull. The ME cuts away the top of the skull, using an electric saw and chisel, and removes the brain. It is sectioned, examined, and sampled.

After the autopsy is completed, any organs exhibiting unusual features are preserved as specimens. The remainder are either sewn inside the body cavity or saved alongside the body until it is released to the next of kin. Samples of blood, urine, stomach contents, DNA, organs, and tissues are preserved or sent to laboratories for further testing. Toxicologists, for example, will test for the presence of drugs, alcohol, and poisons. Evidence obtained during the examination will be sent to the crime lab. Depending on the circumstances of death, the ME may also consult with other forensic experts—such as ballistics, fingerprint, or DNA specialists—about aspects of the case.

The Cause and Manner of Death

The ME's job does not end with the autopsy of the body. He or she must also analyze and interpret the information gleaned from the examination in order to reconstruct the circumstance of the individual's death. Throughout the course of the investigation, the ME aims to determine the identity of the body and the manner, cause, and—if applicable—mechanism of death. He or she will also estimate the time the death occurred. Some of these findings will be entered on the death certificate, and some may eventually be submitted as evidence in a court case.

Identification of the body is often straightforward. The body may have been discovered by a family member or personal acquaintance who can provide the police with the identity. In other cases, the individual might be carrying a driver's license or other photo ID. If the body is too decomposed to be recognizable, it may be identified through birthmarks, scars, or tattoos. Dental and medical records and DNA tests can confirm an identity as well. If there are no leads on a body's identity, the police can send out fingerprints to check against possible matches in databases.

The ME must report the manner and cause of death on the death certificate. Generally, the manner of death falls into one of four possible categories: natural causes, accident, homicide, or suicide. If the circumstances are ambiguous or the body is badly decomposed, the ME may state that the manner of death is "undetermined." The cause of death is the agent that brought about death, such as a gunshot wound or heart disease. In some cases, the ME may specify the mechanism of death—the process in the body that led to death. A gunshot wound may be the cause of death, but the mechanism of death would be the consequences of the wound, such as bleeding, trauma, and other factors.

The exact time of death can be a crucial matter in the investigation of a crime, and estimating it can pose a daunting challenge for the ME. From the moment of death, the body begins to change and decompose. Body temperature cools at a steady, predictable rate. It undergoes rigor mortis, a process in which the muscles of the body initially stiffen, followed by gradual unclenching. Lividity—the gravity-induced settling of the blood in the body after death—also progresses in a predictable manner. There are many other factors that can yield clues about the time of death, such as the filming over of the eyes, the occurrence of insects, and the stage of decomposition of the body. In estimating the time of death, the ME must also take environmental factors into account. If the surroundings are unusually hot or wet, for example, it will affect the body's rate of cooling and decomposition.

The ME describes his or her findings and presents conclusions in the autopsy report. The report draws upon follow-up work, such as lab test results, additional firsthand examination, and research, as well as the autopsy itself. The ME also consults the deceased individual's medical records and the scene investigation report. Many MEs say that this background information is crucial in determining the cause and manner of death. In turn, the autopsy report is critically important in the investigation of a death and, sometimes, in the naming of a suspect and the outcome of a court case. The ME and the staff at the ME's office labor painstakingly to resolve any uncertainties and test and evaluate possible alternative scenarios before finalizing their conclusions and issuing a report.

Chapter 3

Skills, Education, and Training

Even the biggest, most knowledgeable fans of *CSI*-related programming cannot take up a career as a medical examiner on the spur of the moment. In order to become an ME, one must demonstrate a willingness to spend years acquiring the necessary education, exceptional skills, and dedication to the work despite its often grim and gory nature.

For many, a few photos of stab wounds or of an autopsy in process will greatly reduce the lure of the profession. Slicing through skin and muscle and sawing into bone can turn the stomachs of even the least squeamish people. Exposing oneself to a corpse's bodily fluids and possible communicable diseases can also cause one to think twice about forensic pathology. Some may balk at the long training period. But for others, solving the puzzle of sudden or unexpected deaths is a rewarding field of work.

MEs help bring about justice. Their discoveries can lead to changes in public health and safety that can save lives. In some cases, the ME's work can bring closure to grieving families by solving the mystery of how their loved one died.

Skills and Requirements of a Successful Medical Examiner

A passion for science is essential for an aspiring ME. This passion will result in you acquiring the necessary background in biology, chemistry, and physics, and some knowledge of a wide array of relevant sciences such as anthropology, botany, odontology, entomology, and psychology. Unlike MEs on television, a real ME does not personally analyze evidence or perform every DNA test on his or her own. However, in order to work with experts in the fields of trace evidence, ballistics, fingerprinting, toxicology, and DNA analysis and appreciate the results of their lab tests, the ME must have a broad understanding of many areas of forensics.

An ME generally has a keen sense of intellectual curiosity and views challenging cases as scientific puzzles to work out. Unlike police detectives, however, the ME does not speculate about what happened at the scene of the crime. The ME bases his or her conclusions about the circumstances of death solely on the available evidence and his or her own expertise.

The ME cannot afford sloppiness in his or her work. For one thing, the ME's own safety can depend on taking great care in the autopsy process. There is always the possibility that a corpse could be carrying an infectious disease such as HIV, hepatitis, or tuberculosis. If the ME cuts himself or herself with a contaminated

Mechthild Prinz, assistant director of forensic biology for the New York City Office of Chief Medical Examiner, consults with a colleague about the DNA analysis of World Trade Center remains.

scalpel, saw blade, or other sharp object, he or she could contract a potentially deadly disease. Saws used to cut bone create a spray of bone dust and other fine material that could include airborne viruses. Some of these viruses can remain suspended in the air for a long time. For safety reasons, MEs wear gloves, surgical masks, eye protection, surgical gowns, and shoe coverings when they are working in the autopsy room. This protective gear also prevents the ME and his or her assistants from contaminating the body or any evidence associated with the body.

Another reason that the medical examiner must avoid making careless mistakes is that a single error can undermine the credibility of the ME's work and his or her conclusions. For example, an individual's medical history may indicate that she had been diagnosed with a kidney condition while alive. During the autopsy, the ME should observe the abnormal kidney. If he or she fails to notice the condition, it could be interpreted as an error on his or her part. Even if the kidney condition had no relevance to the cause of death, an attorney could use the point to cast doubt on the ME's overall competence and use this doubt to get his or her client cleared of murder charges.

A job in the ME's office is not for the faint of heart. Bodies may arrive dismembered, mutilated, or highly decomposed. The ME cannot allow a sense of squeamishness or disgust to interfere with the examination, even if the body is putrefying or crawling with maggots.

The ME must also find ways of dealing with the psychological impact of encountering tragedy, trauma, and violent crime on a daily basis. For his or her own sake, the ME has to maintain a sense of emotional detachment when working with dead bodies. On the other hand, the ME cannot let this clinical detachment prevent him or her from dealing with the individual's relatives in a sympathetic manner.

Good communication skills are essential for an ME dealing with a grieving family and the many other people connected with

Dr. Jon Thogmartin, ME for Pinellas County, Florida, answers questions about the autopsy results for Terri Schiavo, who died in 2005 after her feeding tube was removed.

the investigation. The family may resent that the ME must perform an autopsy, even when it is required by law. The family may resist the ME's findings. Some cases require cultural or religious sensitivity on the part of the ME. Jewish religious practices, for example, require that a body be buried within twenty-four hours of death. Some Buddhists object to having the body refrigerated. Whenever possible, the ME's office tries to accommodate the requests of the family.

The Body Farm

1
2
3
4
5
6
7
8
9
10
11
12
13
14
15
16
17
18
19
20

On a small piece of property just outside of Knoxville, Tennessee, the casual observer is likely to stumble upon scenes out of a horror movie. Dozens of decaying human bodies may be scattered about the property at any given time. The spot is so famous that it has been mentioned in numerous television shows and movies and was the setting for Patricia Cornwell's well-known mystery novel *The Body Farm*.

The Body Farm, however, is more than a gallery of grisliness. It is actually the University of Tennessee's innovative forensic research facility, where scientists can study the effects of time upon dead bodies. The Body Farm was established in 1971, when forensic expert and faculty member Dr. Bill

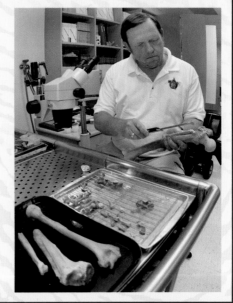

John Williams, director of the forensic anthropology lab at Western Carolina University, helped establish the second Body Farm in North Carolina.

Bass persuaded the university's president to set aside a small piece of university property for studying decomposition. Today's facility covers about three acres, where donated bodies are studied for various lengths of time.

Bass and his assistants study as many scenarios as possible. They may leave some corpses in the open air, while placing others inside car trunks or in shallow graves. Effects may be studied for weeks or even months. During the time that they are monitoring a particular body, researchers gather as much information as they can. They take note of everything from the types of bugs that the body attracts as it decomposes to the way the ground looks after a body has been left there for a while. The wealth of information gathered through research at the Body Farm can help medical examiners narrow down possible times of death and identify factors that could account for specific changes occurring in bodies after death. Forensic departments across the country, as well as the FBI, often go to the Body Farm to carry out their own observations or to get help in pinpointing a time of death.

Working with Others

Along with possessing good communication skills, the ME should be familiar with the ins and outs of government bureaucracy and the legal system. Any given case may involve working with representatives from numerous organizations: the police department and other law enforcement agencies, hospitals, the district attorney's office, and other government agencies such as public health offices. The ME also collaborates closely with other forensic scientists who run the lab tests that result in DNA and fingerprint matches, trace analyses, and ballistics reports. The ME may consult with outside specialists. Within his or her own office, the ME must demonstrate skills as a manager when working with assistants, residents, interns, and technicians.

The ME must also have good writing skills. Although the ME might not consider it "real" work, he or she devotes a great deal of time to completing autopsy reports and filling out forms. The writing in the autopsy report is detailed, descriptive, and highly technical. Since even a minor observation could potentially prove significant later on if the case goes to court, the writing process involves scrupulous double-checking and several levels of oversight within the ME's office. The autopsy report concludes with a brief, nontechnical synopsis of the investigation and the ME's conclusions, written in easily comprehensible language for the use of police officers, lawyers, judges, jurors, and family members of the deceased.

Court Testimony

If the case goes to court, the ME may be called to testify as an expert witness. A "fact witness" testifies about observations and firsthand knowledge of evidence and events related to the case. An expert witness, on the other hand, is qualified to give more

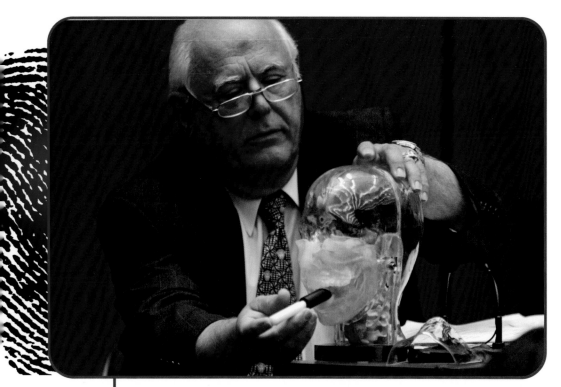

Dr. Vincent DiMaio, a noted expert on gunshot wounds, demonstrates a bullet path during the 2007 murder trial of music producer Phil Spector in Los Angeles, California. His testimony included heated sparring with the prosecutor.

general and broad professional opinions. An expert witness has not necessarily performed the autopsy. He or she may only be speaking from experience, not from firsthand observation of the deceased or the autopsy report.

In court, the ME will begin by presenting his or her credentials as an expert: a degree in medicine and state certification, plus years of training and experience performing thousands of autopsies. He or she may have published research in journals or have considerable past experience testifying in court. At the trial, the fate of the defendant—and the reputation of the ME's office—may depend on the ME's testimony. The ME must be able to explain his or her examination and conclusions in language that the jury will understand. The ME may be asked whether a witness's statement about how an injury occurred matches the evidence. In cross-examination, the defense attorney may try to cast doubt on some of the ME's conclusions, or he or she may merely ask the ME to elaborate on some of his or her findings.

Education and Training

MEs are the foremost authorities on sudden or unexpected deaths. Considering the heavy responsibilities of the job, it is easy to understand why an ME generally completes thirteen to fifteen years of education and training following high school. In order to qualify as a forensic pathologist or ME, one must earn a four-year undergraduate degree and a medical degree, complete years of training in pathology, then complete further training in forensic pathology.

High School and College

Young adults considering a career as a medical examiner can get started immediately by establishing a solid academic background and relevant skills while still in high school. They should take a wide variety of classes in order to achieve a well-rounded education and enroll in honors and advanced placement classes whenever possible, especially in math and science. Students should also work to develop study skills, writing skills, and public speaking skills. They should try to participate in extracurricular activities related to science. Some ME offices offer internships or volunteer opportunities to high school students.

During college, an aspiring ME should concentrate on fulfilling the coursework required for entrance to medical school. He or she may major in science in a premedical program, but not all medical schools require a science major. Some students acquire hands-on experience by working or volunteering in hospitals or clinics.

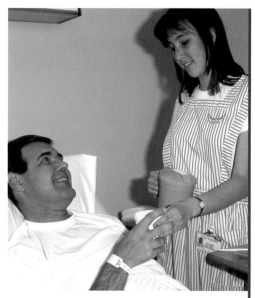

A candy striper helps cheer patients as she makes her rounds. Aspiring doctors can gain experience in health care by performing volunteer work in hospitals, nursing homes, and other care facilities.

Medical School

Entrance to medical school is highly competitive. The admissions office considers grades, scores from the Medical College Admission Test (MCAT), extracurricular activities, and letters of recommendation. Many universities conduct personal interviews with prospective students.

Medical school generally takes four years to complete. Medical students begin by spending most of their time in a classroom taking courses and learning on-the-job skills such as how to take a patient's medical history, examine a patient, and make a diagnosis. During the last two years, students focus more on supervised work with patients in hospitals and clinics. During different rotations, they gain experience in various branches of medicine, such as family practice, surgery, pediatrics, and pathology. In some circumstances, a student can take an elective rotation working in an ME's office.

Residency

After completing medical school, the student is awarded a doctor of medicine (M.D.) or a doctor of osteopathic medicine (D.O.) degree (osteopathic medicine is a form of medical practice that encourages wellness by focusing on health education, injury prevention, and disease prevention). In order to be granted a license to practice medicine, a doctor must complete a residency, in which he or she receives additional training while working at a hospital or other medical facility. An aspiring ME will typically pursue a residency in pathology. The program might include four years of residency in anatomical pathology completed in a hospital, a yearlong residency focusing on clinical pathology in a laboratory setting, and a one- to two-year residency or fellowship in forensic pathology spent in an ME's office.

A doctor's residency—a period of paid, on-the-job training in a hospital or other care facility—is a crucial part of his or her education.

During his or her training period in forensic pathology, the resident will take part in death investigations and perform autopsies under supervision. There's more than one path to becoming a certified forensic pathologist; the doctor may spend a year of his or her training concentrating on toxicology or another related branch of forensics. In order to become certified as a forensic pathologist, the doctor must pass an exam administered by the American Board of Pathology.

Opportunities in the Field

Medical examiners are public servants. Chief MEs are appointed to serve a certain city, county, region, or state. In areas with a large population, they are assisted by several assistant, associate, or deputy MEs. According to the American Medical Association, a forensic pathologist earns an average annual income of $175,000. An ME's actual pay will vary depending on his or her level of training and experience, precise job description, and locality.

The ME's job encompasses more than time spent in the autopsy room and on the witness stand. MEs report their findings to families of the deceased. In some cases, an ME may alert the family to a genetic condition that could affect other relatives. They communicate their findings to insurance companies as well, since an ME's conclusion on a death—whether it was an accident or suicide, for example—can determine whether an insurance company has to pay the family. MEs pass on their findings to various state, federal, and professional organizations. Researchers can use data reported by MEs to compile mortality or crime statistics reflecting trends, patterns, and changes over time. MEs also alert the government and the public to possible threats to public health or safety. In this way, MEs can serve an early warning function, alerting the public to looming health threats.

Teaching

Most MEs do some teaching on the job. There are often interns, students, residents, or volunteers in the office who need to be trained, instructed, and supervised. Police officers working a case frequently observe the autopsies of victims or consult about the significance of the ME's findings.

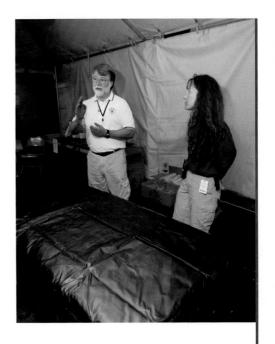

Following the devastation caused by Hurricane Katrina in 2005, Louisiana state medical examiner Dr. Louis Cataldie explains how bodies of victims are placed in body bags before being moved.

In order to be an effective teacher, an ME should be able to communicate on the level of his or her students. Training a resident or assistant in forensic pathology involves a high degree of expertise and a specialized technical vocabulary. Working with laymen without a background in forensics, though, the ME must be able to convey his specialized knowledge in terms that are easy to understand.

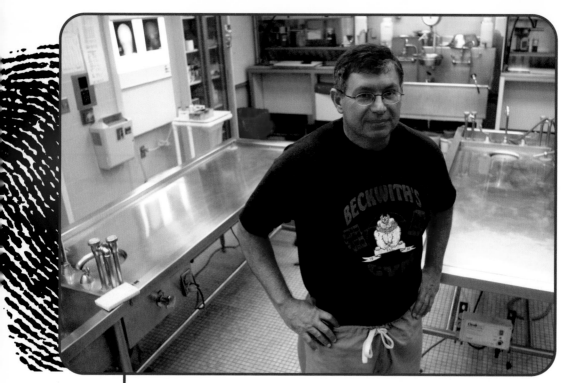

Dr. Stephen D. Cohle, an expert in cardiovascular pathology and sudden cardiac death, stands in the basement morgue where he works as Chief Medical Examiner of Kent County, Michigan.

Research

A career as an ME is a lifelong learning experience. An ME is constantly honing skills and refreshing his or her training in order to keep up-to-date with evolving technology. From time to time, an ME is presented with particularly challenging cases that require a broadening of his or her expertise.

Many forensic pathologists also perform research and become authorities on specific aspects of their field. They may publish their findings in books or articles for journals such as the *American Journal of Forensic Medicine and Pathology*. Some MEs become recognized as authorities in particular areas of specialization. For example, Vincent DiMaio, chief medical examiner of San Antonio, Texas, is recognized as a foremost expert in gunshot wounds. Charles Wetli, former chief medical examiner of Suffolk County, New York, has performed extensive research into deaths due to cocaine abuse. Jan Leestma, former assistant ME at the Cook County Medical Examiner's office in Chicago, Illinois, wrote the authoritative textbook on forensic neuropathology (the study of diseases of nervous system tissue). Stephen Cohle, chief medical examiner for Kent County, Michigan, is a nationally recognized expert on sudden cardiac death.

Consulting

Medical examiners are sometimes asked to lend their expertise to cases outside their jurisdiction. Specialists may weigh in on unusual or sensitive cases. In 2005, for example, a Florida medical examiner asked Dr. Cohle to examine the heart of Terri Schiavo, the comatose woman at the center of an intensely controversial right-to-die case. Dr. Cohle did not find anything abnormal with the patient's heart.

Forensic pathologist Dr. Michael Baden testifies during the O. J. Simpson murder trial. A former chief medical examiner of New York City, Baden has worked on many high-profile cases.

Some charismatic medical examiners or pathologists become media stars who frequently weigh in on high-profile cases. Michael M. Baden, former chief medical examiner of New York City, has investigated the O. J. Simpson murder case, the assassinations of President John F. Kennedy and Martin Luther King Jr., the murder of JonBenet Ramsey, and many more. Cyril H. Wecht, an acclaimed forensic pathologist and former coroner of Allegheny County, Pennsylvania, acted as a consultant in the investigation of the Waco Branch Davidian fire and the suicide of Clinton-era White House counsel Vince Foster.

Though most MEs don't regularly appear on national television, they often have an opportunity to share their expertise. MEs may participate as guest speakers at conferences and seminars related to forensics, law enforcement, or public health.

Clinical Forensic Pathology

Police officers sometimes request that a forensic pathologist examine a living patient, often someone who has been injured during a crime. Because of his or her forensic training, an ME can help with an investigation by interpreting patterns of injuries in a victim. He or she may be able to evaluate whether wounds were intentionally inflicted or if they occurred as a result of an accident. The ME's findings can be crucial in cases in which police are trying to determine if a child has been neglected or abused and in investigations of sexual assault.

Public Health and Safety

MEs contribute to public health and safety by identifying threats such as the outbreak of epidemic disease or a dangerous design flaw in a product. If an ME finds that a deceased individual had been carrying an infectious disease, he or she notifies agencies such as the Centers for Disease Control and Prevention in order to prevent or contain any spread of the disease. When MEs investigate an accidental death, they consider possible measures that could have prevented that death. Data collected by medical examiners and coroners have contributed to the enactment of numerous safety laws. Many of the safety measures we now take for granted—seat belts, child-proof pill bottles, mandatory smoke detectors in buildings—were strongly encouraged by MEs and coroners before they became law.

Chapter

5 | Future Trends

The O. J. Simpson murder trial of 1994 sent shock waves through forensic and law enforcement circles. Regardless of O. J.'s guilt or innocence, the verdict was unanimous on the handling of the evidence. The sloppy investigation of the crime scene offered a shocking example of how errors made by investigators can create doubt among jurors about the prosecution's case and lead to acquittal.

Simpson's lawyers assembled a team of brilliant forensic scientists to testify for the defense, and they were scathing in their evaluation of the police department's performance in handling the evidence. Investigators had neglected to gather all of the useful evidence from the scene. A video showed one criminalist picking up a bloody piece of evidence with dirty tweezers, thus contaminating the sample. Evidence such as hairs, fibers, and samples of bloodstains were improperly stored and preserved. Some investigators on the scene did not wear adequate protective gear such as gloves and hairnets. The police department did not contact the medical examiner until ten hours after discovering the bodies of

Nicole Brown Simpson and Ronald Goldman.

The ME's office was not exempt from criticism. Michael Baden, one of the top forensic pathologists in the country, pointed out over a dozen mistakes made during the autopsy. The ME's worst error was in mishandling the stomach contents of the victims, which cast doubt on his estimate of the time of death.

The uproar over the mismanagement of the evidence in the O. J. Simpson case highlighted the importance of handling evidence properly. Today's crime scene investigators must be much more thorough and much more highly trained than they were in the past. This trend toward a greater degree of professionalism in forensics is likely to continue.

During testimony for the O. J. Simpson murder trial, forensics expert Dr. Henry Lee uses ink to demonstrate blood smear patterns.

The Future of the ME System

The intense spotlight directed on forensic science in the wake of the O. J. Simpson trial and other less prominent instances of

The CSI Effect

When the television show *CSI: Crime Scene Investigation* premiered in 2000, it was among the first programs ever to focus on forensic investigation and solving crimes through science. As *CSI* became popular, other forensic programs appeared, exposing television audiences to laboratories and techniques that past programs rarely showed in such graphic detail.

As a result, the general public is now much more savvy and knowledgeable about the possibilities of forensic investigation. Unfortunately, *CSI* and other shows have also given people a skewed perspective on the capabilities of crime labs and the precision of lab work. Scientists have labeled this the "*CSI* effect." Jurors in criminal cases may disregard evidence because it was not put through the same tests that they saw on television, while families of a

The forensics team on *CSI* searches for a killer. TV shows may influence public perception of forensic investigations.

crime victim want evidence put through unnecessary and expensive lab tests. They have unrealistic expectations about the medical examiner's ability to narrow down the time of death. Police now complain that today's jurors expect every item found at a crime scene to be tested, while prosecutors sometimes quiz potential jurors on their television viewing habits to screen out people who watch forensic shows.

Some researchers, however, feel that the *CSI* effect has been exaggerated. A recent study by University of North Carolina researcher Kimberlianne Podlas presented a mock criminal case to two groups of people. One group watched forensic shows, while the other group did not watch these programs. Her findings showed that television had no apparent effect on verdicts. Juries stocked with *CSI* watchers tended to hand down the same verdicts as those arrived at by non-*CSI* watchers.

sloppy, compromised forensic work could eventually lead to scrutiny of the medical examiner system in the United States. There is a wide variation in standards and organization among ME offices. Some ME offices are independent agencies. Others are part of the police, public health, or public safety departments. Most states require that an ME be a forensic pathologist, but a few do not require any qualifications other than a medical license. There is also a lack of uniformity from one region to another in classification of deaths. The federal government does not have any kind of national ME system. The armed forces is the only federal department that has an ME's office.

An ME's office can establish its reputation for excellence by fulfilling the qualifications for accreditation with the National Association of Medical Examiners. Currently, only about a quarter of all ME offices are nationally accredited. The future will likely see more ME offices applying for accreditation if courts and counties continue to hold death investigators to higher standards.

Tomorrow's Medical Examiner

How will the job change for the ME of the future? In the not-too-distant future, it is possible that the ME will examine the body from a computer monitor, not on the autopsy table. New technology could enable technicians to scan the corpse so that the ME could view a cross section of any particular part of the body. The ME could conduct a virtual autopsy by examining images of injuries and organs. Currently, however, no imaging technology can begin to rival the autopsy in terms of close-up, detailed observation of the body inside and out and accurate identification of cause of death.

DNA analysis and other new technology offer means of shedding new light on old cases. Police have been able to generate possible leads by retesting evidence in unsolved crimes. On the flip side, there have been instances in which prisoners have been able to

A scientist scrutinizes an evidence sample in a lab. Recent technological developments in forensics—particularly DNA analysis—allow investigators to learn far more from trace evidence than in the past.

prove their innocence years after being convicted of a crime. When the case requires the exhumation (unburying) and examination of a body, the ME's office will often be called in to help conduct the process.

As the population grows, the ME's work will gradually increase. There will be a greater need for highly trained death investigators. It will be good for the profession if even a small fraction of today's young *CSI* fans go on to train as forensic pathologists and

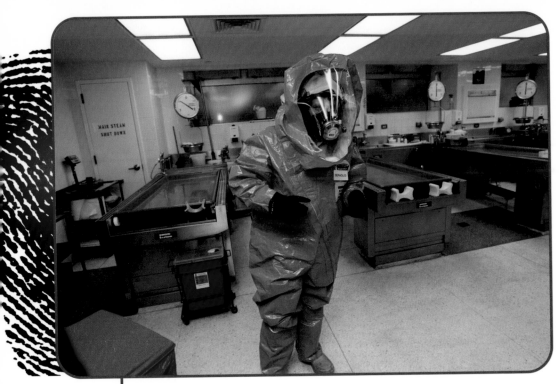

An investigator for New York City's Office of Chief Medical Examiner tests out a Level A hazmat suit, which would provide protection in hazardous environments such as the scene of a chemical weapons attack.

medicolegal investigators. It is important, too, that the government recognize the crucial role of the ME's office. At present, ME offices often have to defend their share of funding at every new round of budget talks. If states and counties want to guarantee that their ME offices will keep doing the best work possible, they must be willing to provide the offices with adequate facilities, equipment, and personnel.

The ME will continue to identify new patterns of death in the bodies that pass through the autopsy room. In the mid-1990s, for example, many large cities saw a surge in violent deaths related to the crack epidemic. More recently, some regions have seen an increase in deaths of illegal immigrants. It is possible that sometime in the future, an ME will identify the first case of avian flu in the United States. The ME's office must also be prepared for the possibility of future mass fatality events, such as terrorist attacks. In some scenarios, a terrorist attack could involve biological, chemical, or radiological (dirty bomb) weapons. If such a disaster does ever occur, the work of the ME's office will be critical in dealing with the aftermath of the crisis.

If your current interest in criminal forensics continues and you put in the hard work of studying and training, you will help solve mysteries, seek justice, spot brewing trouble, tend compassionately to the dead and their loved ones, and ultimately, serve the living and save lives.

anthropology The field that studies the origins of humans and many aspects of human culture.

autopsy The postmortem examination that includes dissection of the body.

ballistics The study of projectiles in motion; specifically, in forensics, the study of firearms and firearms evidence.

coroner An appointed or elected official who investigates deaths not due to natural causes.

DNA (deoxyribonucleic acid) The long molecule found in the nucleus of the cell that carries genetic information.

entomology The study of insects.

exhumation The digging up of something that has been buried, especially a body.

forensic science The application of science to legal matters, criminal and civil.

hepatitis Inflammation of the liver, caused by infectious agents or toxins.

HIV (human immunodeficiency virus) The virus that causes AIDS.

lividity Discoloration of the skin due to the blood settling after death; also called livor mortis.

odontology The study of teeth.

pathology The branch of medicine that explores the nature, cause, and effects of disease.

postmortem Occurring after death.

residency The period of supervised medical training in a hospital following graduation from medical school.

rigor mortis The stiffening of the body after death.

toxicology In forensics, the analysis of drugs and poisons found in blood and other body fluids.

trace evidence Small quantities of physical evidence such as hair, fibers from clothing, soil, dust, and glass.

tuberculosis An infectious disease that attacks the lungs and sometimes other parts of the body.

American Academy of Forensic Sciences

P.O. Box 669

Colorado Springs, CO 80901

(719) 636-1100

Web site: http://www.aafs.org

A nonprofit professional society established in 1948 and devoted to the improvement, the administration, and the achievement of justice through the application of science to the processes of law.

American Board of Medicolegal Death Investigators

1402 South Grand Boulevard

St. Louis, MO 63104-1028

(314) 977-5970

Web site: http://www.slu.edu/organizations/abmdi/

A national, not-for-profit, independent professional certification board that has been established to promote the highest standards of practice for medicolegal death investigators.

American Board of Pathology

P.O. Box 25915

Tampa, FL 33622-5915

(813) 286-2444

Web site: http://www.abpath.org

A member board of the American Board of Medical Specialties that offers certification in pathology.

American Medical Association

515 N. State Street

Chicago, IL 60610

(800) 621-8335

Web site: http://www.ama-assn.org

The doctors' organization dedicated to promoting the art and science of medicine and the betterment of public health.

Association of American Medical Colleges

2450 N Street NW

Washington, DC 20037-1126

(202) 828-0400

Web site: http://www.aamc.org

A nonprofit association of medical schools, teaching hospitals, and academic societies that seeks to improve the nation's health by enhancing the effectiveness of academic medicine.

Canadian Society of Forensic Science

2660 Southvale Crescent, Suite 215

Ottawa, ON K1B 4W5

Canada

Web site: http://www.csfs.ca

A nonprofit professional organization incorporated to maintain professional standards and to promote the study and enhance the stature of forensic science.

Intersociety Council for Pathology Information (ICPI)

9650 Rockville Pike

Bethesda, MD 20814-3993

(301) 634-7200

Web site: http://www.pathologytraining.org

A nonprofit educational organization sponsored by national pathology societies to serve as a central source of information about pathology in the practice of medicine and in medical research and education.

National Association of Medical Examiners

1402 South Grand Boulevard

St. Louis, MO 63104

Web site: http://www.thename.org

The national professional organization of physician medical examiners, medical death investigators, and death investigation system administrators who perform the official duties of the medicolegal investigation of deaths of public interest in the United States.

Web Sites

Due to the changing nature of Internet links, Rosen Publishing has developed an online list of Web sites related to the subject of this book. The site is updated regularly. Please use this link to access the list:

http://www.rosenlinks.com/cif/meex

For Further Reading

Adelman, Howard C., M.D. *Forensic Medicine*. New York, NY: Chelsea House, 2006.

Allman, Toney. *The Medical Examiner.* San Diego, CA: Lucent Books, 2006.

Bell, Suzanne, Ph.D. *The Facts on File Dictionary of Forensic Science.* New York, NY: Checkmark Books, 2004.

Cornwell, Patricia. *The Body Farm*. New York, NY: Berkley Books, 1995.

Hallcox, Jarrett, and Amy Welch. *Bodies We've Buried: Inside the National Forensic Academy, the World's Top CSI Training School.* New York, NY: Berkley Books, 2006.

Lyle, Douglas P. *Forensics for Dummies*. New York, NY: Hungry Minds, 2004.

Rainis, Kenneth G. *Crime-Solving Science Projects: Forensic Science Experiments*. Berkeley Heights, NJ: Enslow Publishers, 2000.

Ramsland, Katherine M. *Forensic Science of CSI*. New York, NY: Berkley Books, 2001.

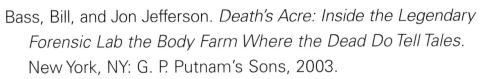

Bass, Bill, and Jon Jefferson. *Death's Acre: Inside the Legendary Forensic Lab the Body Farm Where the Dead Do Tell Tales.* New York, NY: G. P. Putnam's Sons, 2003.

Camenson, Blythe. *Opportunities in Forensic Science Careers.* Lincolnwood, IL: VGM Career Books, 2001.

Christianson, Scott, Ph.D. *Bodies of Evidence: Forensic Science and Crime.* Guilford, CT: The Lyons Press, 2006.

Cohle, Stephen D., M.D., and Tobin T. Buhk. *Cause of Death: Forensic Files of a Medical Examiner.* Amherst, NY: Prometheus Books, 2007.

Fletcher, Connie. *Every Contact Leaves a Trace: Crime Scene Experts Talk About Their Work from Discovery Through Verdict.* New York, NY: St. Martin's Press, 2006.

Genge, N. E. *The Forensic Casebook: The Science of Crime Scene Investigation.* New York, NY: Ballantine Books, 2002.

Houck, Max M. *Forensic Science: Modern Methods of Solving Crime.* Westport, CT: Praeger Publishers, 2007.

Ribowsky, Shiya, and Tom Shachtman. *Dead Center: Behind the Scenes at the World's Largest Medical Examiner's Office.* New York, NY: HarperCollins, 2006.

Ricciuti, Edward. *Science 101: Forensics.* New York, NY: Collins, 2007.

Roach, Mary. *Stiff: The Curious Lives of Human Cadavers.* New York, NY: W. W. Norton & Company, 2003.

Shaler, Robert C. *Who They Were: Inside the World Trade Center DNA Story: The Unprecedented Effort to Identify the Missing.* New York, NY: Free Press, 2005.

Timmermans, Stefan. *Postmortem: How Medical Examiners Explain Suspicious Deaths.* Chicago, IL: The University of Chicago Press, 2006.

Zugibe, Frederick, M.D., Ph.D., and David L. Carroll. *Dissecting Death: Secrets of a Medical Examiner.* New York, NY: Broadway Books, 2005.

Index

A

American Board of Pathology, 23, 39
autopsies, 6, 14, 16, 17–24, 27,
    28–29, 30, 31, 39, 41, 50
autopsy reports, 14, 26, 34

B

Baden, Michael M., 44, 47
Baldridge, Thomas, 22
Bass, Dr. Bill, 32–33
Body Farm, 32–33

C

cause and manner of death, 14, 17,
    18, 24–26
clinical forensic pathology, 44–45
Cohle, Stephen, 43
composite IDs, 12
coroners, 22–23, 45
crime scene, securing, 4, 16
CSI effect, 48–49

D

death certificates, 24, 25
DiMaio, Vincent, 43
DNA tests, 4, 12–13, 24, 25, 28, 34, 50

E

emotional detachment, need for, 30
evidence, collecting/preserving, 4, 5,
    14, 16, 17, 18

F

forensic technicians, 17

H

Hirsch, Dr. Charles, 8, 9

I

identifying bodies, 24–25
    of September 11, 2001, terrorist
        attacks, 11–13

L

Leestma, Jan, 43
lividity, 25–26

M

mechanism of death, 25
medical examiners
    court testimony of, 14, 30, 34–36
    education and training of, 36–39
    future job changes of, 50–53
    job of, 6–7, 14–26, 40–41
    opportunities for, 40–45
    skills and requirements of, 28–31,
        33–34
    television portrayal of, 14, 28
medicolegal investigators, 10, 52

N

National Association of Medical
    Examiners, 23, 50

About the Author

Corona Brezina is a writer working in Chicago. A graduate of Oberlin College with a degree in biochemistry, she has written more than a dozen titles for Rosen Publishing. Several of her previous books have also focused on topics related to science and health, including *Careers in Nanotechnology* and *Nutrition: Food Labels*.

Photo Credits

Cover, pp. 1, 6, 10, 16, 19, 20, 29, 31, 41, 52 © Getty Images; p. 5 © Spencer Grant/Photo Edit; pp. 9, 32, 42 © AP Photos; p. 13 © Tek Image/Photo Researchers; p. 15 © Orjan F. Ellingvag/Corbis; p. 22 © Reúnion des Musées Nationaux/Art Resource, N.Y.; pp. 35, 44, 47 © AFP/Getty Images; p. 37 © Dana White/Photo Edit; p. 39 © www.istockphoto.com/Sean Locke; p. 48 © CBS via Getty Images; p. 51 © Shutterstock.

Designer: Les Kanturek; **Photo Researcher:** Marty Levick